AUDACIOUS IGNATIUS

Written by Paul Mitchell

Illustrated by Katie Mitchell Broussard

audacious (*adjective*): brave, courageous, willing to take bold risks

LOYOLA PRESS.
A JESUIT MINISTRY

www.loyolapress.com

Text copyright © 2018 by Paul Mitchell
Illustrations copyright © 2018 by Katie Mitchell Broussard
All rights reserved.
Published in 2023 by Loyola Press

ISBN 978-0-8294-5803-9
Library of Congress Control Number: 2018958369

Printed in China
23 24 25 26 27 28 29 30 31 32 DC 10 9 8 7 6 5 4 3 2 1

For Andrew, Augustine, Leonardo, and Thomas.

In loving memory of
Katherine Cordes Mitchell,
1925–2018
And for all the Jesuits, past and present.

For more information about becoming a Jesuit,
please visit www.beajesuit.org.

A nobleman's life had Audacious Ignatius.

His love of adventure was simply voracious.

His life about town? Bodacious. Flirtatious.

His style of dressing? Just a touch ostentatious.

Such was the life of Audacious Ignatius.

He loved nothing more than serving his king.
He'd fight any battle. He'd risk anything.

Well, a cannon went BOOM!
And then WHOOSH!
And then CRACK!
Our guy cried, "MY LEG!" as he fell on his back.

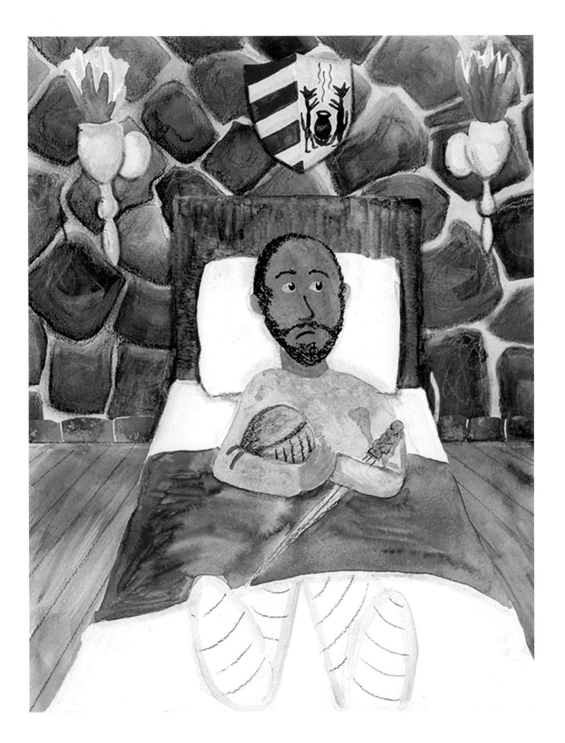

Audacious Ignatius was stuck in his bed.
"My adventures, now, I must live in my head!"

"No matter, I'll dream of superstrong knights
With damsels, adventure, and epic sword fights."

Yet on days when he dreamed of knights and their tales,
He felt great, but later, his spirit would fail.

Our hero then pouted, legs tied in restraints.
"The only book here is of people called 'saints.'"

Ignatius, still skeptical, opened the book.
He was quickly impressed; his defenses were shook.
He decided to give it a much deeper look.

These people *were* knights! Except for one thing.
They did not serve just a temporal king.

But a king most eternal! With hearts full of love,
They served something higher, a Love From Above.

And this Love From Above helped them live here and now.
In giving their lives, they gained riches, somehow.

A heart oh so spacious now burned in Ignatius.
"I must imitate them, with a love most capacious."

"And hey, I've one more book! *The Life of Christ.*
This guy? His message? My heart's so enticed!"

"I'll enter Christ's life through imagine-y prayer.
I'll picture the stories in my head with great care.
Pray for the grace to be open, prepared
For a message of love I can gather from there!"

"Christ's life is the key to the saints that I prize.
His love fills their hearts! He is why they are wise!
How can I give love like these gals and these guys?
I'll write up some steps… a heart and mind exercise!"

"First, know well that I'm loved even though oh so flawed.
Next, spend time with the Lord and walk where he trod.
Offer all I possess, beg for my stony heart thawed,
And act from a deep love, the love that is God."

He tried his new method, and the depth of his heart said,

"Go travel and teach! Serve the poor! Go now! Start!"

He set off across Spain to work as a preacher
To share that, in prayer, the Spirit is teacher
And the Creator, in love, deals direct with each creature.

His teaching grew out of his love of tradition.
Yet, some people thought it a kind of sedition,
And his work ran afoul of the dear Inquisition.

Audacious, Ignatius!" the big men cried out.
"Personal prayer? What is this all about?
Without our control, all will plunge into doubt!
And you're not a priest! You've no clerical clout!"

"Calm down now, my boys. My method's no threat.
It's where my mind and my heart and the Christ have just met!
Just give it a shot. You'll like it, I bet!"

They tried it and loved it! Found graces galore!
Their hearts burned within them like never before!
"Audacious Ignatius! Develop this more!"

Our hero thanked them, traveled north and then east
To Paris for a mind, heart, and cultural feast,
And started training to be a Catholic priest.

"I need some companions," now thought Ignatius.
He gathered a team, thoughtful, kind, perspicacious.

They took vows to be, from self-centeredness, freed,
To spread the Good News in both word and in deed,
And lovingly give what the Church and world need.

And as the years passed, the company grew
All over the world! They amassed quite the crew.
In Africa, Asia, and the Americas too!
And, if you dare... the story can include you!

For if, like our hero, you learn how to pray,
Plans to live with deep love will come right your way.

And if, on some days, these plans seem too audacious,
Say, "God, give me a heart just as bold as Ignatius."

Also Available

THE EXAMEN BOOK

PB | 978-0-8294-5127-6 | $14.99

To Order:

Call **800.621.1008**, visit **store.loyolapress.com**, or visit your local bookseller.